Sin No More:
My Journey to Freedom

Minister Rosby L. Glover

Protective Hands Communications

Riviera Beach, FL

copyright© 2013 Rosby L. Glover
All rights reserved

ISBN 978-0-9892028-6-2
Library of Congress Control Number: 2013938778

No part of this book may be reproduced, stored in a retrieval system, or transmitted in any form or by any means, electronic, mechanical, photocopying, recording, or otherwise without the express written permission of the author.

Published by
Protective Hands Communications
Riviera Beach, FL 33404
Toll free: 866-457-1203
www.protectivehands.com
Email: info@protectivehands.com

Printed in the United States of America

Contents

"Until you do right by me …"	1
No More Excuses	9
Let's Talk About Demons	19
What Can God Do For You?	27
The Road to Recovery	41
Self-confrontation	49
C.H.A.N.G.E.	57
Mom, I Miss You	66

"He who the Son sets free is free indeed!" John 8:36

ACKNOWLEDGEMENTS

This body of work could not have been done without the quiet support and encouragement of my wife, Kimberly Lynne Glover; she is truly my help meet. For over 30 years God has maintained and strengthened this union through a series of falls, failures and family issues.

Kimberly, I realize your strength and resolve has allowed me to focus on things that really matter and because of you, I'm a stronger man. I am forever grateful and I love you so much!

To my children, Kedra, Adam, Christopher, Ryan and Rosalynn, thanks for allowing me the opportunity to show each of you the power of God's love. Each one of you have meant so much to me throughout my life. I couldn't have asked for any more talented, resilient, loving, caring, humble and supportive children.

To Clarence, Beulah, Ronnie and Glenice, thank you for making the sacrifice each of you made so many years ago. You exhibited the spirit of love and compassion at a time when we needed it the most.

Charles, JoAnn and Jerome, the power of prayer is

often times not acknowledged, but I know your prayers helped sustain me during some very difficult times. I love all of you.

Finally, to Reverend C. J. and Etta Mae Glover, although you've both gone to live with the Lord, the upbringing you gave to me as the "baby" of the family was truly a testament to the love both of you had for God. I thank Him for entrusting little old me into your hands.

Daddy, you made sure I got a college education because you saw the importance of it even though you didn't possess a high school diploma.

Momma, because of your love for me I am able to love Kimberly even more. Most of all, you showed me how powerful the love of God is. You taught me to always trust Him, to always seek God's will and to always follow Him, regardless of what others would do.

For many years I did not heed those words, but I never forgot them. Momma, I loved you so much that I decided to write a poem about you on Mother's Day, 2011. I have included it in this work so others can know the power of a God-fearing mother. Until we meet again.

Rosby

Chapter One

"Until you do right by me ..."

And Jesus said, *"Neither do I condemn you; go and sin no more."*

Those powerful words were spoken by Jesus to the woman, who according to the scribes and Pharisees had been caught in the act of adultery, a very serious charge which carried the penalty of being stoned to death. However, their motive was not necessarily to mete out justice, but rather to have something of which to accuse Jesus. But instead of answering them, Jesus stooped down and wrote on the ground with his finger, literally ignoring them.

They continued to badger Jesus in an accusatory tone. "What are you going to do about this?" they asked.

Jesus simply responded, "He who is without sin among you, let him throw the first stone." That's when the game changed.

Can't you see them standing there, pointing the finger at each other. 'You throw it, man.' And the other responds, 'I can't throw it because I have sinned in the past.'

Isn't it funny how we can scorn, ridicule, and even accuse others of failing to live right until the spot light begins to shine on us? Then we simply do like the Pharisees and fade into the back ground.

This particular scripture is of extreme interest to me because several years ago, after fasting and laying before God in prayer, I was essentially told the same thing. *Go put your family back together again, and sin no more!*

At the time, I was in a recovery facility in Central Florida after hitting what can only be described as rock bottom. There I was, a man who just a few years earlier was a deputy warden at a prison and just a few months before that, I was director of operations at a drug treatment facility. But now I was in the midst of the very criminal element I once had the authority to watch over. Though I have never been arrested or charged with a crime in my life, it was only by the grace of God that I had the opportunity to live with those who had.

I must admit I felt a bit uneasy at first. After years of telling people when to get up, when to shower, when to eat, those same instructions were now being given to me. But I remained grateful to God for allowing me to be alive and I remained focused on my family, who were now torn apart. My uncanny ability to sensationalize the obvious had finally caught up with me.

A Downward Spiral

My downward spiral began after I lost my job with the Corrections Cabinet. It was a job I loved, but a job that didn't love me. Had I remained at that job, I would have lost the one thing that mattered to me more than anything, other than God, and that's my family. It was an unforgiving occupation that allowed me to witness the divorce or separation of countless friends simply because their spouse couldn't understand the tremendous amount of stress they were under. I was headed down that same road until God intervened.

One night after drinking and partying with my friends, I came home to a woman scorned. My wife and I had only been married about 4 years at the time, but she said something to me that night that I shall never forget. 'Until you do right by me, you will never prosper.'

I don't think she realized it, but those words seemed to start a dreadful decline in my life that lasted for several years. I was forced to look at who and what I had become and I wasn't pleased. I had become defiant and I refused to admit that she was right, but my defiance led to a severe decline in every aspect of my life.

I dismissed my wife's remarks as that of a young lady who simply wanted more attention. So I continued my partying ways and literally ignored her; if not physically, certainly mentally. I was always the light of the party and I wasn't about to let anyone, including my wife, dim that light for me.

While my partying life increased so did my wife's prayer life. While she was praying that God would save our marriage, I was brooding over what she had prophesied over me earlier, *'Until you do right by me, you will never prosper.'* Those words were reverberating in my head.

Eventually, I lost my job at the Corrections Cabinet and began working for a rent to own company. Because of my ability to sell a blind person a newspaper, I was very good at my new job. I was quickly promoted from the collections department to assistant manager. I was headed back to the top, baby!

It was about that time when I was introduced to the *big C — crack cocaine*. I vividly remember how a member of my wife's family turned from being a friend to my supply man. It was both interesting and fascinating because his regular job earned him more money in three days than I was earning in 2 weeks. He stood ready to buy and I stood ready for the free supply.

My supply man would routinely come to my store

and wait for me to close so we could go and make a drug purchase. At first, it was innocent enough; he wanted company and I didn't mind getting free cocaine.

After the nightly cocaine purchase we would go to his house where he'd break my portion off and then he would cook the rest. You see, he always cooked his cocaine into crack rock and smoked it, but I was not about to do that because I'd heard that crack cocaine was addictive. Fortunately, he never pressured me to join him.

However, during our many trips to purchase drugs I began to notice that he appeared to be enjoying a more extreme high than I. So one day he purchased a large quantity and offered to give me my usual lines to snort, but that day I told him to cook it all. It was a monumental decision because that was simply the beginning of my end.

I had made the decision to smoke crack cocaine and the rush that I received when I inhaled crack for the first time assured me that I would never be snorting cocaine again. It had to be rocked up for me.

It's needless to say, but in a short period of time, feeding my addiction became more important than feeding my family. Still, I was a functional addict. I held down a job, attended church, sung in the choir, became a church trustee and even Deacon Pro-Tem.

However, deep inside of me I knew what I was doing was wrong and somehow I had to get away from my destructive life.

Well, the opportunity came when the store I was managing was sold to another company. Shortly thereafter, I came across notes left behind by the Area Manager. The notes indicated that I was only in their short-range plans; just long enough to train my replacement. Of course, I confronted the company about my findings and was immediately terminated. Wow! Another job lost. What do I tell my wife? After all, we have three children now and another on the way.

After weeks of not being able to find work, my prayer was answered. Remember, I said I wanted to get away and my chance had finally come. I was offered a manager's position in Nashville, Tennessee, three hours away from Louisville and only five hours from my hometown.

A Prayer Answered or A Curse?

Nashville was supposed to be the new start we were looking for. After all of the bad things that had occurred in Louisville, it was time to put it all behind us and start anew. Only one problem with my *new* start — I was still the old me! Simply put, all of the baggage I was carrying, lying, cheating and drugging came right along with me. The bible says beware of wolves in sheep clothing and I had become a wolf.

It seemed the only place I could find a reasonable place to live was near the store where I was training. Unfortunately for me it was smack in the middle of the hood where drugs were readily available. It wasn't long before I found those who could discreetly supply my needs. Soon, discretion turned into detriment. My family began to worry about me. Even when I talked on the phone, my mother, father and brothers could hear that I wasn't the same.

One brother, the one that always checked on me, after hearing the change in my voice, decided to drive to Nashville and see for himself. He brought my mother with him. What he suspected was quickly confirmed upon their arrival.

Instead of finding me in a large home in a pristine neighborhood as he was accustomed to; he found me in a filthy, two bedroom apartment in an undesirable neighborhood. My mom was shocked, but not judgmental; she was always that way with her boys. How-ever, it was obvious something was wrong. My mother and brother endured the stay, but left knowing that I was not the same person they had known just a few short months ago.

What started out as a promising move quickly evolved into a nightmare. I found that living in a drug infested neighborhood where you were seen as an opportunity, brought short-term gratification, but long term ramifications. I met people who were willing to feed my addiction for free. But you know it wasn't free, right?

In fact, it carried major consequences had the Lord not watched over me. You see, my house had become the cook house. One night, we cooked more cocaine than I had ever imagined was possible. In fact, it was that night when I realized I had bitten off more than I could possibly chew, and if there was a God, I needed Him now! I prayed that God would intervene and that He would do so quickly. I had to C.H.A.N.G.E. *

Chapter Two

No More Excuses

My oldest brother and his wife decided to renew their wedding vows for their 26th wedding anniversary. They invited me and my family down to Florida to participate in the celebration. Of course, I made every excuse as to why we couldn't be there. After all, I was the master of excuses. But for once, the excuses were all eliminated, it was time to face reality.

I arrived in Florida noticeably frail, but yet the same charismatic person I've always been, so any suspicion of substance abuse was readily erased. The event was a lovely one, but I knew I had to C.H.A.N.G.E.* so I came armed with my résumé as a desperate cry out for help. That help came in the form of a man named Louie Wainwright, Jr. I truly believe that God placed this man in my life to help save my life.

Mr. Wainwright was a unique individual to say the least. Very laid back, but genuinely warm, approachable and caring. When I interviewed for the job at the Drug Treatment Center he was operating, I did so with little or no expectations. In fact, the position was a downward move from my usual level of work. But to my utter surprise, I was offered a much higher position.

Not really expecting to be hired, I wasn't prepared to start anytime soon. But how do you tell someone like Louie that you were only testing the waters?

I told him how grateful I was, but I would have to go back to Nashville and close out some things, therefore I couldn't start immediately. His response totally surprised me.

"I can wait," he said. "What do you need, thirty or sixty days? The position has been open for quite some time because I've been waiting for the right person and you are that person."

Wow! Look at God work. This was my time to get things right, to leave those demons back in Nashville and start anew with my family; so I thought.

A month later, I arrived in Florida with all of my possessions, which I must admit wasn't much. I'd sold almost everything of value to support my habit. So there I was with my luggage and all of the baggage of my addiction. I was thinking I would defeat this thing once and for all. After all, I'm *working* at a drug treatment center. How many of you know that wherever you go, you take your baggage with you? So I

10

can tell you it wasn't long before things began to deteriorate.

I soon gained access to the same type of people I thought I had left in Nashville. I deliberately left my wife and family in my home town with my mom as I prepared to make this change. But what I realized was no change could occur without first dealing with the demons within.

My demonic experience was one that could have torn my family apart. But in some adverse way it actually made us stronger in the long run. What man meant for evil, God reversed it for His good. What a mighty God we serve!

Family, Faith and The Father

I must admit that I come from a closed-knit family where we were taught to always separate the person from the behavior. So if anyone took a fall from grace the family was there to help restore that person back to health. I needed all of the restoration and grace that could be mustered because my habit had simply gotten out of control. It was at that time that I experienced tough love for the very first time. The secret was out about my addiction and my oldest brother along with the brother that was closest to me finally confronted me.

In typical addict fashion, I denied that I had a

problem and I insisted that *my only problem* was them coming to my house insinuating that something was wrong.

Now these were two men of God, one a senior pastor at a much respected church and the other an up and coming minister. Yet I had no problem lying to them about my situation. I was in complete denial. (Someone once said that denial stood for: **d**on't **e**ven **n**o [sic] **I a**m **l**ying).

Fortunately for me, my oldest brother knew there was one person I could never lie to and the next day that person was at my front door.

My second oldest brother had taken the liberty to drive my mother all night long down to Florida so this issue could be brought to light once and for all. All of the brothers knew I had a special bond with my mother. I was the last of the five boys, the youngest in the family, and she let everyone know that I was *her baby!* She often told me the story about the time when the doctors informed her that either she or I would not make it through her delivery as she was not supposed to have any more children. But my mother prayed for me and God brought both of us through. I loved my mama and I was not about to lie to her about anything.

I remember that day like it was yesterday. First my closest brother arrived, and then my oldest and second oldest brother and my sister-in-law and finally my mother entered the house. The confrontation began earnest enough, we opened up with prayer and then the case was presented against me. I got the opportunity to apologize to my family and for the first time, the opportunity to admit I had a problem that I couldn't handle on my own. We closed the meeting with a plan and a prayer.

After everyone left my house, I wanted so badly to get a crack rock, but I had to meet my family later for dinner. I hugged my wife and confessed the help we needed was finally coming. After all, I had become someone she didn't know. If there was a saving grace in all of this, it was that our children were too young to know what was happening.

God moved mightily that day, but soon after my family left I found myself going back to the familiar place of escape I had come to know.

One night, a few weeks after the family meeting, I accused my wife of stealing from me and I actually threatened her with a knife. I had truly lost it. I had become someone that I didn't know, someone my wife didn't know and my family didn't know. It was that moment that caused my wife to leave and seek help.

My brothers came and said the time had come for me to get the professional help I needed. I agreed to go to the nearest detoxification facility. Once there, I was encouraged to seek further treatment.

Remember Mr. Wainwright, the angel that God put in my life? Well, it was at the lowest point in my life that he reached out to pick me up. I knew I didn't deserve any help from him. After all, I had let him down when he needed me, but Mr. Wainwright didn't see it that way. He made arrangements for me to get free treatment from one of the *out of town* facilities that was part of the network of facilities I had previously worked. What a real man he had become in my eyes. I couldn't understand it then, but he taught me so much about not giving up on people.

So here I am at a treatment facility with convicted addicts. First, they wanted to know what crimes I was charged with committing. I simply told them I had allowed myself to be overtaken by demons. Soon they stopped asking about my charges, they wanted to learn more about the demons I spoke of.

As part of our daily routine, we had to attend group sessions. I would tell the group members how crack cocaine was a demonic spirit and my group leader would dismiss it as simply Mr. Glover's belief. He'd tell his groups that I thought crack cocaine was a demon. He on the other hand had never used drugs, but wanted to tell me as an avid user what I didn't know about the demonic effects of crack cocaine. Soon the class dismissed him and wanted to know more about my belief.

God began to use me as a powerful instrument to help those who needed it the most. My faith went to another level. I started a nightly prayer meeting in my dormitory. Soon men from other dorms would come to our dorm for prayer before going to bed. I realized I had reached the lowest point in my life and the only way I was going to rebound was by asking God to restore me.

After two months of witnessing to a countless number of men and lying before the Lord daily, God answered my prayer. Just as he told the woman in John 8:11, 'Go and sin no more,' He spoke very loud and clearly to me those very same words. He said, 'Rosby, go get your family back together and sin no more!'

I promised God that if He would deliver me from the demonic spirits that had me bound, I would tell the world how great He is. I've tried to uphold my end of the deal because He has surely upheld his.

God began to bless me in ways unimaginable once I submitted to His will. When I told my brother what God had spoken to me, he consulted the experts who advised him to leave me where I was because enough time had not elapsed. I reiterated to him that I had to do what God had clearly spoken to me and if he wouldn't come get me, I would find away back home.

Obviously, he heard the seriousness in my voice and he upheld his end of the bargain and picked me up. Remember, I was not under any sentence or criminal proceedings; I was just blessed to be there with those who were.

When I returned from my stay in the facility, my brother reminded me that God would restore the years the locust had eaten. I was blessed to receive my old job back as an assistant to the maintenance engineer. Yes, I was an assistant to the janitor, but this was no ordinary janitor. This was a man that taught me more about life as I worked with him than I had learned in all of my college years. I'm still grateful to Frank Shropshire for pouring into my spirit.

Upon my return home, God began to bestow tremendous blessings upon me and my family. My wife found work in her field of study. God blessed us with a car that was rusted throughout, but it had great tires and a not so decent engine. God gave me favor with some mechanics at the church and they kept it running for us.

At that time we were living in a two-bedroom apartment. Our four children shared one bedroom and my wife and I the other. In spite of everything, we were one happy family. Soon God answered my prayer again and allowed us to rent a three-bedroom house with a large, fenced in yard and fruit trees. It was during this time that God told me to use my degree and leave the comfort of my janitor's job.

I was blessed with a number of people that God placed in my life and eventually I was able to work for a private company as a therapist, thanks to one of those individuals. After being with that company for six months, they blessed me with a brand new company car. God is really beginning to show out now.

Soon thereafter, we bought our first home. It was a four bedroom home with a large family room, fenced in yard, and many other amenities. The kids were growing into their own, my wife was receiving promotions on her job; heck, I even received promotions on my job and became *State Director of Foster Care* for the company.

However, I soon realized that it was time for me to move on. It was a career move that didn't make sense to me or many other people, but it was what God had spoken into my spirit. One thing I had learned to do over the years was to obey the voice of God.

I went to work for the ministry established by my brother and I am still with that ministry to this very day. I went from program manager to director of programs to executive director, which is the position I serve in today. Wow! What a journey!

My sojourn involved a very loving and dedicated family, a tremendous increase in my faith in God, and love from a very faithful Father who declared that He would never leave me nor forsake me and He never has. Glory to God!

You may not be blessed with a loving, dedicated and caring family and your faith in God may have been waning, but I encourage anyone that is fighting a demonic spirit to experience the faithfulness of the Father. God can surely deliver you if you'd only let go and let God! But first you must know something about demons. Let me share with you what God showed me concerning this matter of demons.

Chapter Three

Let's Talk About Demons

Let me establish something from the beginning. This chapter is not attempting to argue one's theological stance on demons. The widely held opinion is that if you are saved, demons can't live in your body. Some theologians opine that The Holy Spirit and demons can't coexist in the same body.

Another viewpoint is that everyone has demons in their lives. That position points to the fact that there are no scriptures that say Christians can or cannot have demons. In fact, many believers in the Bible had to deal with demons. A clear understanding of demons is that they are *things* that controls, harasses, torments, or drives you to do what you ought not to do or wish you didn't do whether you are saved or unsaved. I tend to gravitate towards that argument.

Demons get into our minds and control our will and emotions. Demons, however, cannot get into your spirit because that is where Jesus resides. The point I'm making is simply this, we have all sinned and come short of the glory of God. As sinners many of us have had to deal with some demons in our lives. I was no exception.

I'm not talking about telling a little white lie every now and then, I'm talking about the kind of demons that cause you to stay out all night long when you know you should've been at home. I'm talking about the kind of demons that cause you to spend all of your money on a bad habit rather than paying bills and feeding your family. I'm talking about the kind of demons that will have you blinded by lust for another man or woman, even when you've got the best partner you could ever have at home waiting for you.

I'm talking about the kind of demons that keeps you at the card table instead of at home at the dinner table. I'm talking about the kind of demons that will make you steal someone else's belongings even when you didn't have to. The kind of demons that attacks your mind and no matter how hard you try to pull away from its grip, it literally pulls you deeper and deeper into its grasp. Demons that come, *but to steal, kill and destroy one's life.* The kind of demons I'm talking about are the kind of demons Jesus spoke about in the bible.

Jesus used the expression *"unclean spirit"* three times in the Bible (Matthew 12:43; Mark 5:8, and Luke 11:24). Each time He used this expression, He did so within the context of making reference to a demon.

The Greek word for spirit is *pneuma* which was also used to mean daemon, which were supernatural beings otherwise known as demons. A close study of the way Jesus used the expression discloses that He spoke within the context of demons that inhabit the body. That is demonic possession.

In fact, the expression *"unclean spirit"* appears ten times in the New Testament. In the plural form it also appears ten times. Also, there are variations of the expression that appear in the bible. (e. g. spirit of an unclean devil, Luke 4:33; and foul spirit, Rev. 18:2). Whenever this expression is used in the Bible in reference to a disease or people, it is used within the context of possession.

Have you ever had to deal with a family member caught up in drug addiction or alcoholism? Drugs like heroin, crystal meth or crack cocaine. These drugs have literally destroyed families, friendships, even entire communities.

If you are honest with yourself, you'd probably have to admit that there have been times when you wanted to throw in the towel, wash your hands of the addicted brother or sister and walk away. If you are like most families, you couldn't keep anything in the house of value because every time you looked around, something was missing. The TV, DVD player, cable box, microwave oven, you name it! You became a prisoner in your own home and you were confused.

The paradox of this issue is the fact that the person who was addicted couldn't understand why they weren't able to tear away from the drugs. They didn't consider themselves to be bad people. They attended church and on the outside it appeared as if they had it all together. But when the church benediction was given, they would go back and dwell among pornography, alcohol, illicit sex, lying, jealousy, envy, all kinds of dead stuff. Yes, they were *in* the church, but they were bound by the chains of sin.

Often times, people come into the church engulfed by a legion of demons. These individuals are seeking help, but in many churches, the people have a tendency to talk about the person, instead of helping them. They talk about how pitiful the person looks, how they ought to be ashamed of themselves, but they offer little or no help.

The people in the church will say things like, "It seems to me that they ought to want to help themselves. They're just pathetic."

But the bible declares in Galatians 6:1, "Brethren, if a man is overtaken in any trespass, you who are spiritual restore such a one in a spirit of gentleness, considering yourself lest you be tempted."

I truly believe that the vast amount of people simply underestimate the power of demonic spirits.

My addiction was not a cigarette addiction or even a marijuana addiction. In my mind, I could quit smoking cigarettes at anytime and I actually did it. But with drugs, despite the fact that they were taking a tremendous toll on my body, I had to understand that it was more than a physical addiction.

Although, my drug addiction had me crying all night long, it wasn't emotional. The need to use drugs originated in my mind, yet it wasn't mental. I was engaged in *spiritual warfare.*

According to the Apostle Paul, there's only one way to fight in the spiritual realm. Paul says you must put on the whole armor of God. You've got to gird your waist with truth. Put on the breastplate of righteousness. You must shod your feet with the preparation of the gospel of peace. Take the shield of faith with you along with the helmet of salvation and the sword of the Spirit, which is the word of God. After doing all of that, Paul encourages us to pray.

I've come to realize that many people, whether they are dealing with an addiction to crack cocaine, alcoholism, sex, shopping, or the like, they want to change, but they just don't know how. I can tell you from experience that it's very hard and I can tell you why.

In the Gospel, according to Matthew 12: 43-45, the bible declares, "When an unclean spirit goes out of a man, he goes through dry places, seeking rest and finds none. Then he says, I will return to *(insert your name here)* house from which I came. And when he comes, he finds it empty, swept, and put in order. Then he goes and takes with him seven other spirits more wicked than himself, and they enter and dwell there: and the last state of that man is worst than the first. So shall it be with this wicked generation." (NKJV).

I believe what Jesus was saying is simply this. When you stop using drugs for a short period of time, on your own, you get a feeling of accomplishment, but you fail to fill the void in your life with the word of God, so your unclean spirit (demon of choice) comes back to revisit you.

The spirit finds you swept clean, and put in order, but still empty, so he, along with seven of his buddies decide to pay you a visit and before you know it, you relapse. However, this time your habit is stronger than before because you are now dealing with eight demons instead of one. Your condition is worst than it has ever been. That tells me that while we are playing, we should be praying, because we need to realize that we're dealing with demons.

In my opinion, that's why AA (Alcoholics Anonymous) and NA (Narcotics Anonymous) and some of those other A's don't work for some people. They're simply trying to fight the wrong battle. I've heard countless people refer to themselves as grateful recovering addicts. Though I applaud their effort at recovery, it appeared to me that at some time during your life you should be proclaiming victory.

I see it as a matter of the heart. Proverbs 23:7 states, "For as a man thinks in his heart, so is he." So if you continue to think that you are always in a perpetual mode of recovery, you will never recover. It's also a mind issue.

Paul says in Romans 12:2, "And do not be conformed to this world, but be transformed by the renewing of your mind..." He says in II Corinthians 5:17, "Therefore, if anyone is in Christ, he is a new creation; old things have passed away; behold all things have become new." I, further prescribe to John 8:36, "He who the Son sets free, is free indeed." Are you beginning to see my point?

Chapter Four

What Can God Do For You?

Perhaps, you're thinking that all of this spiritual material sounds good, but you consider yourself too far gone. Well, the reason I've been challenged to write this work is specifically for people like you. People who in all aspects of life are good people who made bad decisions. I was no different.

Earlier, I wrote about some of the ways God manifested himself mightily in my life. I even told you how he blessed me with a great career, even in my addiction. I was one of the biggest abusers of drugs, while at the same time, I was Director of Operations at a drug treatment facility.

Early on in my career, I subscribed to the posture of do as I say, not as I do. Why do you have to do what I tell you to do? I had the power and because I said so! What a selfish and Napoleon type attitude to have. So yes, my life took a downward spiral. Your life does not have to take the same course, if you prescribe to the contents of this book.

What can God do for you? The same thing He did for me and my family when the enemy was trying to tear us apart.

The bible gives us a perfect example of how to deal with our demons in Mark 5: 1-20. In that passage, we read about a man who was dealing with a legion of demons and how he was able to overcome the demons and most importantly, it shows how you can do the same.

Please tolerate my presentation as I get a little sermonic in this prescribed solution. The first thing that you have to do to overcome your demon is, *"Wait on the Lord!"*

In chapter 4 of Mark, Jesus was teaching the multitude from the boat. Then he said, 'Let's go to the other side.' Before they could get there, a storm came. (How many times have we needed a blessing from Jesus, but instead a storm came?) Jesus calmed the storm that they encountered and he can calm your storm if you just wait on Him.

The Bible declares that as soon as Jesus got out of the boat, a demon-possessed man immediately met him. This man knew he needed to be restored and delivered from the demons. He also understood that he needed to be delivered from his surroundings, from his situation and from himself. This man didn't just need any deliverance, he needed a divine deliverance that could only come from Jesus. He waited on the Lord and now was his chance. The next thing he did was to *"worship the Lord."*

After Jesus commanded the unclean spirit to come out of the man, the next thing Jesus did was to ask the man his name.

"My name is Legion," the man answered.

You see, when you are demon possessed, you're not just who your parents named you, you're a lying, cheating, dishonest, distrustful, stealing, cunning, carnal, conniving, conspiring, malicious, plotting, begging, paranoid, dangerous, dysfunctional individual! In other words, you are full of many demonic spirits and every evil spirit has to leave you and go elsewhere when Jesus cleans you up. That's why you have to be careful who you hang with because there may not be any swine nearby when the spirits are being exorcised from you.

You see, there comes a time in your life when no matter how hard you try to make it on your own, no matter how much you depend on family, you have to come running to Jesus and worship Him!

No matter how far you feel you've strayed in life, no matter how many demons have possession of your body right now, Jesus can speak a word and they have to run. They simply can't stay in His presence.

Demons tremble and fall.

When we worship God, He reveals Himself. When we worship God, He fulfills his promise. When we worship God, He releases His blessings. When we worship God, He begins to do a work in our lives.

According to the bible, after the man was all cleaned up, Jesus told him to go home to his friends and tell them what great things the Lord had done for him, and how Jesus shows compassion. We must witness for the Lord, eagerly telling others about His goodness.

But here's what the people did. You'd think that once Jesus cleaned this man up, a man who was cutting himself and living in the graveyard, the people would rejoice. Instead the people got scared and asked Jesus to leave.

Your experience may be the same. Once people see what Jesus has done for you, they're going to ask you or Jesus to depart. They won't be able to relate to you anymore. As long as you were in a dysfunctional state, they knew how to deal with you. They could ignore you, they could use you, they could manipulate you, and they could even make fun of you. But now that you're clothed in your right mind, they don't know how to handle you, so they ask you to leave. That's why some relationships crumble after your deliverance. Some people won't know how to deal with you.

I'm glad Jesus told this man to go home to his friends and tell them what great things the Lord had done for him and the compassion the Lord had shown him. This is where many of God's people miss the mark.

This man wanted to go with Jesus, but Jesus told him to go home and witness. God cleans many of us up and we go back home and witness, but many choose to go elsewhere and start *"testi-lying"* and now those people are being exposed.

When you are delivered from your demons, do whatever Jesus tells you to do. If He tells you to start a homeless shelter, do it. If He tells you to start a soup kitchen, do it. If He tells you to be still, then be still. Jesus told me to get my family together again and sin no more; I try everyday to make a *habit* of doing just that.

Speaking of Habits

Many times when we think of habits, we think of people who smoke, drink alcohol or do drugs. We simply tend to put a negative connotation on the word, *habit*. We often say, he's got a bad habit of drinking or she's got a bad habit of cursing. Seldom do you hear people saying someone has a good habit of anything. We don't say he's got a good work habit.

We just say he loves to work. We don't say that she has a good habit of going to church, we say she loves going to church. So we have a tendency to make habits synonymous with negative or bad things.

A habit has been defined as a constant, often unconscious inclination to perform an act, acquired through its frequent repetition. Habit applies to any activity so well established that it occurs without thought on the part of an individual. In other words, it's something that you do over and over again without thinking about it.

2 Peter 2:19 says, "For by whom a person is overcome, by him also he is brought into bondage." The NIV says, "For a man is a slave to whatever has mastered him." The Living Bible says, "For a man is a slave to whatever controls him."

So my brothers and my sisters, this habit thing goes far beyond drugs and alcohol. Some people are slaves to work and to gossip. Others are slaves to another person's opinion. Peter says you are a slave to whatever has mastered you. I'm proclaiming whatever has mastered you is a habit.

You must understand that good people are bound by bad habits. But many people rationalize that if they admit to having a habit, they are somehow less spiritual. But God would say to you, don't let your habits affect your holiness.

You see, if you don't handle your habits, they can turn into hardships. Hardships can make you lose heart. There's a story about tiny Cumberland College in Lebanon, Tennessee, who on October 7, 1916 was losing a game to powerful Georgia Tech, 220-0 when one of the Cumberland players fumbled the ball. He looked at his teammate and said, 'Pick it up,' to which his teammate responded, 'You pick it up, you fumbled it!' So hardships can make you lose heart. But hardships can also make you persevere.

There's the story of a boxer who got knocked down in the first round, got back up and went to his corner. 'You've got him right where you want him,' his trainer told him. 'He hasn't laid a glove on you yet.'

The boxer responded, 'I'm going to go back out there, but you keep an eye on the referee, because someone is beating the mess out of me in that ring.' We have to persevere in our struggles.

Often times, God uses our struggles to shape our character, alter our course, or put us in a position to benefit others in ways that we cannot see during our time of difficulty. The songwriter puts it this way, 'We will understand it better, by and by!'

When we run away from our problems, we are running away from what God is doing in our lives. We can expect God to continue bringing us into these circumstances until we learn what he is trying to teach us.

My daddy use to sang an old familiar hymn, '*A charge to keep I have, a God to glorify, a never dying soul to save and fit it for the sky. To serve this present age, my calling to fulfill, Oh may it all my powers engage to do my Master's will.*'

We have a charge to endure hardships and conquer our habits. We have a charge to keep our focus in all situations. We have a charge to help our fellow man. We have a charge to take care of our families. We have a charge to raise our children in the fear and admonition of the Lord. We have a charge to support our church. We have a charge to clean up our community. Simply put, we have a charge to keep.

God is at work in your life. You may not recognize it or understand it, but He's in the storm with you. He's calling you to be like Peter and be a water-walker, not a boat person. In other words, keep your eyes on Him during your storms.

Like you, I have gotten weak at times, but I'm reminded of what Jesus told Paul, 'My grace is sufficient for you, for my strength is made perfect in weakness.'

Isaiah puts it this way, "But they that wait on the Lord shall renew their strength; they shall mount up with wings as eagles; they shall run, and not be weary, they shall walk, and not faint.'

Many of us fail to recognize that God is in charge. We take our hardships and our habits into our own hands. After we've made a mess of things, we want to give it back to God. My mother would always tell me to take my burdens to the Lord and leave them there. *If you trust and never doubt, he will surely bring you out. Take your burdens to the Lord and leave them there!*

My brother always says we've got to learn to trust God, even where we can't trace him. Those were simple words of encouragement, but powerful in their resolve for me to sin no more.

I'm often reminded that storms will come in your life and it's during these times when we have to recognize that we are not in charge. When our storms come, we have to be like an eagle.

An eagle will fly to some high spot and wait for the winds to come. When the storm hits, it sets its wings so that the wind will pick it up and lift it above the storm. While the storm rages below, the eagle is soaring above it. The eagle does not escape the storm. It simply uses the storm to lift it higher. It rises on the winds that bring the storm.

When the storms of life come upon us we can rise above them by setting our minds toward God. After all, it's not the burdens of life that weigh us down; it's how we handle them. But our problem is that we have an *Invictus* mentality. Some of you may have heard or read the following poem:

> *Out of the night that covers me*
> *Black as a pit from pole to pole,*
> *I thank whatever gods may be*
> *For my unconquerable soul.*
>
> *In the fell clutch of circumstance*
> *I have not winced or cried aloud.*
> *Under the bludgeonings of chance*
> *My head is bloody, but unbowed.*
>
> *Beyond this place of wrath and tears*
> *Looms but the Horror of the shade,*
> *And yet the menace of the years*
> *Finds, and shall find, me unafraid.*
>
> *It matters not how strait the gate*
> *How charged with punishments the scroll.*
> *I am the master of my fate:*
> *I am the captain of my soul!*
>
> * William Henley

Invictus is known as a good poetic piece, but in my

opinion, it's wrong. You're not the master of your fate or the captain of your soul.

The word *Invictus* means "unconquered." According to the author, *William Henley*, no matter how a person lives his life, good or bad, a man is his own god and can manage his own destiny without any need of instructions from a creator.

Unfortunately, that's the posture many of our children take today, and as a result we have more of our boys in prison than in college. We have more of our girls struggling with their sexuality then ever before. It's because we've allowed our habits and our hardships to affect our holiness. We have to recognize our charge.

The writer of Hebrews in chapter 12, verse 14 tells us to pursue peace with all people, and holiness, without which no one will see the Lord. Think about this passage just for a moment. *Without holiness, no one will see the Lord.* That puts some pressure on us as Christians.

Paul tells us in Romans 12:1, 'I beseech you therefore brethren, by the mercies of God, that you present your bodies a living sacrifice, holy, acceptable to God, which is your reasonable service.' He goes on to say, "and do not be conformed to this world, but be ye transformed by the renewing of your mind, that you may prove what is that good and acceptable and perfect will of God." That's our charge.

I understand that habits can lead to hardships and our hardships tend to make us want to quit. I've been there myself. But how many times does the word of God commend hardship for the Christian?

Over and over, the scriptures tell us that difficulty and hardships have redeeming value for those who walk in faith. The word of God tells us that by faith Abel offered to God a more excellent sacrifice than Cain. It is by faith that Enoch was taken away so that he did not see death. It is by faith that Noah built an Ark for the saving of his household. The list goes on. We need not give up when hardships come our way and of course, many of our habits lead to hardships. But we can still look up and receive the fullness of God's greatest blessings.

It's in the midst of hardships that God works to build the highest and best for us. Look at every character in the Bible and you will find that many had unhealthy habits and had to endure hardships, particularly those who received God's blessings.

The Hebrew boys, Shadrach, Meshach and Abednego, had their fiery furnace experience. Daniel had to deal with his den of lions. Joseph went from the pit to Potiphar's house, to prison and then to the palace. Peter was sent to prison. John was exiled to Patmos. David fled from Saul and Samson had his eyes put out.

I Peter 5: 8-11 tell us to, "Be sober, be vigilant; because your adversary the devil walks about like a roaring lion, seeking whom he may devour. Resist him, steadfast in the faith, knowing that the same sufferings are experienced by your brotherhood in the world. But may the God of all grace, who called us to His eternal glory by Christ Jesus, after you have suffered a while, perfect, establish, strengthen, and settle you. To Him be the glory and the dominion forever. Amen."

Many of you reading this book have tried to live holy lives, but your habits keep getting in the way. You've tried to be set apart, but hardships keep getting you down. But don't let your habits or your hardships affect your holiness. As someone once said, watch your thoughts; they become words. Watch your words, they become actions. Watch your actions, they become habits. Watch your habits, they become character. Watch your character, it becomes your destiny.

If you want to live holy lives, try Jesus. If you want to stop your bad habits, try Jesus. If you want to deal with your hardships, try Jesus. I am now a living witness of what God, through His son Jesus and the unction of the Holy Spirit can do to eradicate your unhealthy habits if you turn it all over to Him.

Chapter Five

A Self-help guide that blessed me

Those of us recovering from emotional problems and addictions sometimes feel empty or we have a longing that needs to be fulfilled. Although we have given up on addictive behaviors as the solution to our problems in living, something may still be missing. Understanding our feelings is often a confusing task, since many of us have taken care to keep ourselves numb, seeking to deaden our feelings, rather than feeling distressed. So how do we sidestep our feelings of shame?

Some of us have avoided looking too closely at ourselves for fear of what we might find. Others of us have almost unknowingly refused to accept ourselves and instead often negate our self-worth through endlessly comparing ourselves to friends, acquaintances, and family members. Still others of us have attempted to rebuild these feelings of shame through rigid perfectionism.

The Origin of Our Shame

Feelings of shame stem from negative self-evaluations that undermine our self-confidence. Often these self-evaluations are rooted in childhood experiences in which we were not nurtured with a high sense of self-worth and self-respect. Thus we reach the false conclusion that we were and are of little value or worth.

Some of us gravitated towards negative self-evaluation in response to the painful effects of addiction. The more we tried to quit using drugs, and the more our efforts failed, the more we devalued ourselves. Some of us act as if we were born predisposed to think negatively of ourselves and our abilities. Although we may achieve a number of important goals, in our minds, we never seem quite good enough.

While shame may stem from different causes or sources, we can help ourselves to feel better, accept our self-worth, and enhance our self-confidence by taking charge of our thoughts, feelings, and behavior.

We must examine some of our negative self-evaluations and explore ways to change our thoughts and behaviors. Since our shame often leaves us feeling numb or fearful of our emotions, let's begin by increasing our self-awareness.

Feelings are sensations resulting from our mind-body connection. Oftentimes, one word is all we need to label our emotions. There are four words that can cover the range of our feelings – *sad, mad, glad, and scared* – but many of us use different words such as *pissed off* or *numbed out* to describe our feelings.

An Exercise Just for You:

Use the space provided to describe how you are feeling now.

- Right now, I feel:

  _____

- Next, think about the times that you have been aware of your feelings of shame. Some of us describe these feelings in terms of feeling empty, sad, numb, or unable to feel anything. The following exercise will help you get started:

- For me shame feels like

  _____

- I first became aware of my feelings of shame when

  _____

- The last time I felt a surge of shame was?

  _____

- Now, I feel shameful when

  _____

Feelings of shame are unpleasant in and of themselves. In addition, shame can keep block us from making changes needed to live healthier, happier lives. When we feel intense shame over a long period of time, an urge often accompanies the discomfort: "I felt so ashamed that I wanted to hide."

Feelings create urges → Urges motivate behavior.

Our shame may cause us to feel an urgency to reduce our pain, but often in self-destructive ways. Sabotaging a relationship, isolating ourselves, hurting ourselves, compulsive drinking or eating, or having sex to avoid our feelings of shame are all examples of behaviors that dull the pain, but fuel a continued sense of shame. Take a few moments and list under the headings *Helpful* and *Harmful,* some of the things you've done to stop your feelings of shame. Reflect on some of the things that have been helpful as well as those actions that were eventually harmful.

Helpful	Harmful

Learning To Change Our Thinking

Let's continue by taking a closer look at some of the beliefs we hold about ourselves. When we put ourselves down, we are usually evaluating ourselves negatively. These self-evaluations are made up of our own thoughts and beliefs about ourselves. Thoughts are how we communicate with ourselves. Our feelings are largely based on our sense of shame. When we put ourselves down through our negative self-evaluations, we are actually telling ourselves that there is something basically wrong with us. It isn't that we have made mistakes or that bad things have happened to us, we tell ourselves that *we* are the mistake, we are bad.

Here are some examples of negative self-evaluations, sometimes called shame-based logic.

"My mother always told me I wouldn't make it, and she was right. What a loser I am."

"I'll never measure up. The more I try, the more inadequate I am. Everyone must know by now how utterly worthless I am."

"This lasagna is disgusting. I'm a lousy cook."

Think for a moment and then write two of your own examples of shame-based logic.

1.

2.

Our put-downs, our shame-based logic, our negative self-evaluations, are all distortions of reality. They are myths about us. Therefore, we can empower ourselves and reduce our feelings of shame by disputing our myths, challenging our shame-based logic, changing our negative self-evaluations, and ending our self-imposed put-downs.

We dispute our logic by actively questioning our beliefs about ourselves. We attack our shame-based thinking by demanding proof or evidence to substantiate our beliefs. We question our negative self-evaluations and scrutinize our expectancies. We stop rating ourselves and our worth. Instead, we accept our value as a worthwhile, fallible person who deserves to be treated with dignity and respect.

When confronted with an addiction the first thing to do is confront yourself. And the way to confront yourself is to deny yourself. In denying oneself, the addicted person is literally putting off self-will and making a determination to follow Jesus.

The way to follow Jesus is to believe what John 1:1 says, "In the beginning was the Word, and the Word was with God, and the Word was God." As someone once said, "Belief in the beginning is the beginning of belief."

An in-debt look at things the addict must do reveals the following:

1. Deny self – Put off self-will and determine to follow Jesus. *Matthew 16:24-25*

2. Abide in the Word – Continue in His Word as a true disciple. *John 8:31*

3. Love one another – Love as He does and we will be known as His disciples. *John 13:34-35*

4. Pray – Pray with thanksgiving and we will have peace that the world cannot give or takeaway. *I Thessalonians 5:17; Philippians 4: 6-7*

5. Be a doer of the Word – Hear, do, continue, blessed. *James 1:22-25*. Teach, reprove, correct, train, equip. *II Timothy 3:16-17.*

6. Seek to please God in all things. *John 8:29, Romans 8:8, II Corinthians 5:9, Ephesians 6:6-7; Philippians 2:13-14; Colossians 1:10; I Thessalonians 2:4; 4:1; Hebrews 13:21; I John 3:22*

7. Develop and use spiritual gifts – Seek and begin perfecting the gifts. *Romans 12:3-8; I Corinthians 12 and 14; Ephesians 4; I Peter 4:7-11.*

8. Disciple others – Jesus has received *ALL POWER!* We can go in His name teaching others what we learn. *Matthew 28:18-20.*

9. Learn to counsel scripturally – God will make us

competent and loving counselors. *Romans 15:14; Colossians 3:16.*

a. Learn to listen. Be prudent and wise, learning to listen. *Job 34:3; Proverbs 18:2, 8, 13, 15, 17-18.*

Question and instruct – Lovingly help in the put-offs and put-ons. *Ephesians 4:15; II Timothy 2:24-26.*

Chapter Six

Self-Confrontation

"See to it that no one takes you captive through philosophy and deception, according to the tradition of men, according to elementary principles of the world, rather than according to Christ." (Col. 2:8)

Self-confrontation is one of the hardest things an individual can do. We often get so wrapped up in masking who we are, and of course, the effects of mind-altering drugs complicate our view of reality. Often we don't know who we truly are, making it even more difficult to confront the true self. However, if we seek wisdom through the word of God, He will give us insight. *Lean not on your own understanding. In all your ways acknowledge God and He shall direct your path.*

Mankind has invented many theories concerning man's problems and the solutions to those problems. However, God has provided His word, not as a help or inconvenience or support, but as His authority for all life and all living. From it we may learn how to have abundant life beginning in this life.

We must develop sensitivity to sins, failures and shortcomings. Most importantly, we must admit our shortcomings, face them squarely and repent; hence, self-confrontation.

If we listen to the Word and do not do it, we begin to delude and deceive ourselves. When we hear the Word applied to our problem, we must act on it. If we become an effective doer of the Word, we shall be blessed in what we do. God has promised it.

In James 1:22-25, it reads, "But be doers of the word, and not hearers only, deceiving yourselves.[23] For if anyone is a hearer of the word and not a doer, he is like a man observing his natural face in a mirror; [24] for he observes himself, goes away, and immediately forgets what kind of man he was. [25] But he who looks into the perfect law of liberty and continues in it, and is not a forgetful hearer but a doer of the work, this one will be blessed in what he does." NKJV (NLT) Don't miss your blessings!

To truly understand the affects relapse can have on one's ability to stay clean, we need to look no further than the book of Matthew, Chapter 12: 43-45. In the passage, Jesus says these words, *"When an unclean spirit goes out of a man, he goes through dry places, seeking rest, and finds none. Then he goes and takes with him seven other spirits more wicked than himself, and they enter and dwell there; and the last state of that man is worse than the first...."*

Imagine if you will, that in your case, the unclean spirit is your drug of choice. You've stopped using for a while (dry drunk), so you think you've actually gotten clean. However, there is a void when you are not using alcohol or other drugs and that void must be filled by the Holy Spirit. When you fail to fill that void, the demon that left you (your drug of choice) revisits your mind and finds that you've only been abstinent for a while. So he brings with him seven other demons more wicked than him. That's why it's not unusual for your habit to increase after a time of abstinence or dryness, because you are dealing with more than one demon. Makes sense, doesn't it?

During my time in treatment I was taught to be aware of relapse signs. Some of the most prevalent ones are listed below:

Denial – The same denial during cocaine use, "I can quit anytime I want to" or "I'll just smoke marijuana." As I mentioned earlier, DENIAL means **D**on't **E**ven **N**o [sic] **I A**m **L**ying!

One Hundred Percent Convinced I'll Never Use Again – One day at a time just doesn't seem important anymore.

Defensiveness – Defensive when talking about your problem or treatment.

Compulsive – Overworking and/or compulsive about activities and over extending yourself.

Impulsive – Acting without thinking; in many cases a reaction to stress.

Loneliness – Isolation, avoiding other people. Feeling alone. An old proverbial saying is, "An addict alone is in bad company."

Tunnel Vision – Looking at only one part of your life. It could be a good area, creating a false sense of well-being and security or a bad area, emphasizing feelings of being treated unfairly by other people and a victim of bad luck.

Depression – Flat feeling, sometimes over sleeping goes along with it; not talking about feelings or depression.

Loss of Planning – Wishful thinking instead of realistic planning.

Plans begin to fail – Plans begin to fail because of the lack of a plan, not following through on the plan or trying the impossible.

Wishful thinking – Concentration replaced by fantasy.

Easily angered – Periods of anger, frustration and irritability.

Irregular eating habits – Over-eating and under-eating, not eating regular meals, eating junk food instead of healthy food.

Irregular sleeping habits – Can't sleep; restless nights, then sleeping too long from exhaustion.

Progressive loss of daily structure – Not keeping up with routines and then having long periods of time with nothing to do and feeling bored.

Self pity – 'Poor little old me' attitude.

Rejection of help – Cutting yourself off from your support system (family, friends, co-workers, etc.)

Thoughts of social use of drugs – Thoughts of using in a controlled fashion.

Driving past drug dealer's house – Stopping in the old neighborhood to say hello.

Large amounts of money in your possession – Carrying large amounts of money near the weekend.

Conscious lying – Rationalization gets so bad the addict sees it but feels as if he/she can't stop it.

Controlled using – Trying to use just a little regularly or go on a short binge just to celebrate.

Loss of control – Return to heavy using.

Ungratefulness – When one begins to think people owe them something instead of being grateful for what they have.

Unforgiving – Refusing to forgive others even though

God has forgiven you

To be successful in quitting any addictive substance or addictive behavior, you must find the reasons for quitting that are right for you. You must pinpoint why you want to stop. It could be for health reasons, family reasons or spiritual reasons, what matters most is that you quit.

Although your family, friends, co-workers and employer may insist that you stop your habit, stopping for someone else won't keep you away from your addiction for very long. You may temporarily quit for other people's reasons, but if you are to permanently abstain, it must be for your reasons only. Use the pressure being put on you by others as an opportunity to discover your own reasons for getting clean and sober.

Like most people who develop problems with addictive substances, you probably feel ambivalent or have conflicts about giving up your addiction. This is perfectly normal considering that all addictive and compulsive behaviors involve conflicting desires. Part of you loves your addictive behavior while another part of you hates what you've become. Adding to this conflict is the fact that your memory of your drug related experiences may be selective. You may remember the "bell ringer" you got during your first hit, but you may have forgotten the low points that came afterwards. Those times when there was no money for groceries, no money for bills, nothing to show for a week of pay?

It's called euphoric recall, the tendency to vividly remember the highs, while forgetting the lows. Furthermore, you may still be holding on to the fantasy that you can somehow learn to control your substance use, actually believing that you can quit whenever you desire. It's not hard to see how these and other factors can create strong conflict and mixed feelings about giving up your substance or drug of choice.

It's a huge mistake to pretend that these feelings of ambivalence don't exist. Admitting that you have conflicting thoughts about your drug of choice doesn't mean that you lack the commitment and determination to follow through on your plan of being set free. Instead, it shows your willingness to confront reality head on.

People who rigidly refuse to acknowledge or talk about their feelings of ambivalence are often putting themselves at a higher risk for relapse. This suggests that those who don't confront their ambivalent feelings are likely to act them out in self-defeating ways.

Jesus tells us in Matthew 6:24 and Luke 16:13 that. *"no man can serve two masters; for either he will hate the one and love the other; or else he will hold to the one and despise the other..."* The choices are up to you, but believe me a decision has to be made.

I recall facing the same dilemma during my early days of recovering. It wasn't easy because I had grown to like my feelings of euphoria, being able to escape and avoid who and what I had become, but I hated the down-side. I realized that I didn't know who or what I had become.

It was during those times that I needed my family the most and yet I knew that I wouldn't be in a position to take care of them, if I continued down the road of relapse. That's when the Spirit pointed me to Matthew 12:43-45. I read that passage, I marinated in it and I let it get deep in my spirit. It was then that the vision became clear and I remember breaking into a praise dance because I knew that God had truly delivered me.

In other support groups they encourage you to remember your anniversary date; the date you begin your recovery. But God spoke a different word to me. 'Your sins have been forgotten,' He said. 'You need to forgive yourself and forget what you use to be in order to be what I have predestined for you to become.' Therefore, I don't remember the date or the year; I just remember that one day, quite sometime ago, God delivered me. Glory to God!!!!

Chapter Seven

C.H.A.N.G.E.

Upon hearing my mandate from God to get my family back together again and sin no more, I knew I had another charge to keep. I had to let others know about the delivering power of Jesus Christ. At the blessing and encouragement of my pastor, Rev. Dr. C. E. Glover, the one who very passionately and scripturally saved my life, the C.H.A.N.G.E. Ministry was started at our church.

The C.H.A.N.G.E. Ministry was initially founded to help family members in the congregation who had a son, daughter, uncle, aunt or other relative with a drug or alcohol problem. However, it was soon realized that the scope of the problem extended to not just family members, but church members. There were an increasing number of church members with substance abuse issues that wanted and needed a spiritually based foundation. Many felt they had nowhere else to turn, but to God. They had tried abstinence, relocating, hospitals and clinics, but they had not tried God. They needed to change their lives to line-up with God's character.

3 John 11 states, "He that doeth good is of God, but he that doeth evil hath not seen God."

As the twelve steps believe that a power greater than ourselves could restore us to sanity (Higher Power), we recognize God as that "Higher Power."

The Bible tells us that he who the Son sets free is free indeed (John 8:36). Therefore, the C.H.A.N.G.E. Ministry, using a model I developed called *the Psycho-Spiritual model to recovery* recognizes the essence of this scripture. The premise is simple, if Jesus (The Son) has delivered you from your chains of bondage (addiction) and because of His grace and mercy, you are free indeed. Why then, do people continue to refer to themselves as *"recovering?"*

As the model's name indicates, *the Psycho-Spiritual* Model is made up of two distinct, yet unique parts – the Psycho (mind) and the Spiritual (Greek [pneuma] – the rational soul). This simply implies that the addicted person must really put in his/her soul and spirit so that God can truly free one from their addiction. Once again, I am reminded of Paul's words to us in Romans 12:2, "And do not be conformed to this world, but be transformed by the renewing of your mind, that you may prove what is that good and acceptable and perfect will of God."

The mind has been programmed with natural *established attitudes*. These are the beliefs, thoughts, ideas, opinions, convictions, prejudices that we have concerning ourselves, others, objects, activities and even God. These attitudes were formed by our parents, the educational system, and society — in short, our experiences.

Whatever you hold in your mind will tend to occur in your life. If you continue to believe as you have always believed, you will continue to act as you have always acted. If you continue to act as you have always acted, you will continue to get what you have always gotten. If you want different results in your life or your work, all you have to do is change your mind.

The late Eleanor Roosevelt, former First Lady of the United States once said *"Great minds discuss ideas; average minds discuss events, small minds discuss people."* However, when you allow your mind to be altered, it's almost impossible to become great.

"You can chain me, you can torture me, you can even destroy this body, but you will never imprison my mind." (Mahatma Gandhi)

God *wants* us to change. He wants us to be delivered and set-free from the bondage of addiction. However, there are some things you must confront in order for your rational soul and your mind to receive the freeness that God is bestowing upon you. Indeed, it begins with a belief in yourself and most of all a belief in God. Let go and let God!

Let go of the dark, which you wrap yourself in like a straight jacket and let in the light. *Jesus is the light of the world!* Stop trying to protect, rescue, judge and manage the lives around you. Your children's lives, the lives of your husband, your wife, your friends because that is what you are powerless to do. Remember, the lives of other people are not your business. Their lives are their business. They are God's business. Even your own life is not your business. It's also God's business.

Matthew 6:31-33 states, "Therefore do not worry, saying, What shall we eat? or What shall we drink? or What shall we wear? For after all these things the Gentiles seek. For your heavenly Father knows that you need all these things. But seek first the Kingdom of God and His righteousness, and all these things shall be added to you."

Leave it to God. It is an astonishing thought. It can become a life-transforming thought and only He can help you *change!*

The Bible is filled with scriptures designed to help you live an addiction free, God fearing life. So why do so many people succumb to what the world has to say relative to addiction and relapse, instead of what God has to say through His Word?

I have come to recognize that the propaganda and clichés you hear in secular venues may be more harmful than helpful, if you are not spiritually fit or equipped to recognize the tactics of the enemy. So my intent, when writing this book is to provide you with the armor necessary to win the spiritual battle of addiction by recognizing and confronting self, then allowing God to do the work.

To the many addicts who found recovery in some sense through the teachings of AA, NA and other support groups, my sincere blessings are with you. This writer believes that bringing the Steps and the Scriptures together makes sense for several reasons. First, the 12 Steps are based on biblical principles and were written at a time when AA's primary spiritual source materials were the Bible and the teachings of a Christian organization known as the *Oxford Group*. Second, just as the 12 Steps are a "spiritual" rather than a "religious" program, the Bible is a spiritual rather than religious book. The Bible does not tell us what church to join or what brand of theology to subscribe to. It provides spiritual truth that we must apply to our own lives and recovery.

The spiritual concepts behind the 12 Steps appear throughout the Bible. Here is a small sampling of passages that support each step. As you read through them, think of them less as "proof texts" and more as "connecting links" between the Steps and the Scriptures, between recovery and faith. Let's take a closer examination. Taken from the *Recovery Devotional Bible.*

- *The Twelve Steps of A.A. and Their Biblical Comparisons*

We admitted we were powerless over our addiction – That our lives had become unmanageable.

"And I know that nothing good lives in me, that is, in my sinful nature. I want to do what is right, but I can't." Romans 7:18 (NLT)

Came to believe that a power greater than ourselves could restore us to sanity.

"Let every soul be subject unto the higher powers. For there is no power but of God..." Romans 13:1 (KJV)

Made a decision to turn our will and our lives over to the care of God as we understood Him.

"Then He said to the crowd, If any of you want to be my follower, you must turn from your selfish ways, take up your cross daily, and follow me." Luke 9:23 (NLT)

Made a searching and fearless moral inventory of ourselves.

"Let us search and try our ways and turn again to the Lord." Lamentations 3:40 (KJV)

Admitted to God, to ourselves and another human being the exact nature of our wrongs.

"Confess your faults one to another, and pray one for another, that ye may be healed." James 5:16 (KJV)

Were entirely ready to have God remove all these defects of character.

"If ye be willing and obedient, ye shall eat the good of the land." Isaiah 1:19 (KJV)

Humbly asked Him to remove all our shortcomings.

"Humble yourselves before the Lord and He will lift you up in honor." James 4:10 (NLT)

Made a list of all persons we had harmed and became willing to make amends to them all.

"First be reconciled to thy brother and then come offer thy gift." Matthew 5:24 (KJV)

Made direct amends to such people wherever possible, except when to do so would injure them or others.

"Give and it shall be given unto you; good measure, pressed down, and shaken together, and running over, shall men give into your bosom. For with the same measure that ye mete withal it shall be measured to you again." Luke 6:38 (KJV)

Continue to take personal inventory and when we were wrong, promptly admitted it.

"Because of the privilege and authority God has given me, I give each of you this warning: Don't think you are better than you really are. Be honest in your evaluation of yourselves, measuring yourselves by the faith God has given us." Romans 12:3 (NLT)

Sought through prayer and meditation to improve our conscious contact with God as we understood Him, praying only for knowledge of His will for us and the power to carry that out.

"Let the words of my mouth and the meditation of my heart be acceptable in thy sight, O Lord." Psalm 19:14 (KJV)

Having had a spiritual awakening as a result of these steps, we tried to carry this message to alcoholics, and practice these principles in all our affairs.

"Brethren, if a man be overtaken in a fault, ye which are spiritual, restore such a one in the spirit of meekness; considering thyself, lest thou also be tempted." Galatians 6:1 (KJV)

In conclusion, this model of recovery is not salvation in some final sense, but rather a catalyst for one to experience salvation in a deeper, real-life situation as one allows Christ to free them from their addiction.

God revealed to me through His Spirit that I had allowed demonic spirits to take resident in my temple. I had allowed them to affect my thinking, my drive, my intellect and ultimately my mind. He revealed to me that the mind was the devil's playground. I had heard that expression many times in the past but never knew its true meaning until it became the epic center of my battle. Paul reminded the Roman church that they should not be conformed to this world, but they should be transformed by the renewing of their minds. That's the posture I'm presenting to you today. You must renew your mind in order to overcome the evil spirits that are produced by illicit drugs. Free your mind and all other parts of your being will follow!

S.I.N. NO MORE!

Stop the Ignorance Now!

Mom, I Miss You!

Dedicated to the memory of Etta Mae Glover

It's that time of year again,
That time that makes me cry;
Yes, it's Mother's Day
But I never said goodbye!

Mom, you were the glue, that held our family;
So many sacrifices you made, many of which people didn't even see
You made sure we had a hot meal to start the day afresh
And when our school day was over, with a hot dinner we were blessed

You then toiled long hours, from evening to early morn you worked;
All because you had 5 boys, whom you loved until it hurt;
I was the youngest, "That's my baby," you would so proudly call.
The one you prayed so heavy for, especially when I had my fall!

Thanks to your prayers, I got back in the race
I still see that beautiful smile of yours, every time we would meet face to face.
It seems they don't make moms anymore, with the qualities you bestowed
You were truly an angel sent by God, to touch many hearts and souls!

Mom, I miss you and I know I always will.
We shared a very close bond, which was stamped with God's seal;
Clarence, Charles, Jerome and Ronnie, they all miss you too;
So Happy Mother's Day from all of us, we wouldn't be who we are today without you.

We all remember that dreaded day in March of '97;
That day when you were called to take, your rightful place in Heaven;
I cherish the time, that God allowed us to spend together;
No one can ever take that away; those memories will be with me forever.

For those of you who still have your mother, love them with all of your heart
As a matter of fact today, yes this Mother's Day, is a good time to start!
Pray that your mother, follow the way of the cross;
Because with everything that's happening these days, it's so easy to be lost.

And for those of you out there that has lost a mother too
Please allow me to say, these simple words to you;
Just believe that Jesus was born of a virgin, died on the cross, and rose for our sin;
And if your mother was saved, like our mother was, you will see her again.

Mom, I miss you!